TOM THUMB
AND THE
FOOTBALL TEAM

Pippa Goodhart

Illustrated by
Philippe Dupasquier

OXFORD
UNIVERSITY PRESS

Great Clarendon Street, Oxford OX2 6DP

Oxford University Press is a department of the University of Oxford.
It furthers the University's objective of excellence in research, scholarship,
and education by publishing worldwide in

Oxford New York

Auckland Bangkok Buenos Aires Cape Town Chennai
Dar es Salaam Delhi Hong Kong Istanbul Karachi Kolkata
Kuala Lumpur Madrid Melbourne Mexico City Mumbai
Nairobi São Paulo Shanghai Taipei Tokyo Toronto

Oxford is a registered trade mark of Oxford University Press
in the UK and in certain other countries

British Library Cataloguing in Publication Data

Data available

ISBN 0 19 919598 6

1 3 5 7 9 10 8 6 4 2

Mixed Pack (1 of 6 different titles): ISBN 0 19 919601 X
Class Pack (6 copies of 6 titles): ISBN 0 19 919600 1

Printed in Hong Kong

Contents

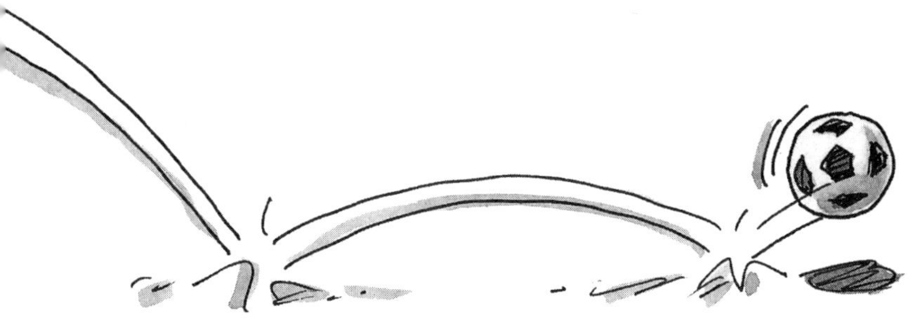

Chapter 1

One Teeny-Tiny Child

There was once a man who loved his wife and he also loved football.

His wife loved the man and their home. But what she really wanted was a baby to love.

She longed for a baby as you or I might long for a drink on a hot day.

The woman said to her husband,
"Just one teeny-tiny child would make
me happy."

And, believe it or not, that's exactly
what the woman got. She gave birth to
a teeny-tiny baby boy.

"We'll call him Tom," said her
husband. "Tom Thumb, because he's
no bigger than my thumb."

The woman wrapped her teeny-tiny
baby in her best cotton hankie. She cut
the end of the finger from her finest
pair of gloves to make him a bonnet.
She tucked Tom into an eggshell cradle
and she was happy.

Well, the years passed as years do. And Tom's mother did what mothers do. She cooked for Tom and sewed for Tom and taught Tom to crawl and walk and talk.

But as Tom grew from being a baby to being a boy, he grew to wanting more than cuddles and pretty clothes and nice food. He wanted friends and fun. He wanted to find out about the world.

Chapter 2
Let Me Out!

"I'm bored," said Tom to his mother one day. He was kicking currants all over the table.

"Well," said his mother. "If you'll stop spoiling those currants you can see how I make a nice pudding for your father's dinner. Sit on my thimble and watch what I do."

But there's not much fun to be had
in watching a spoon being stirred
around above your head. Tom wanted
to see how the flour and eggs and
milk all mixed together inside
the bowl.

So, when his mother turned to put
a pan of water to boil, Tom reached his
teeny-tiny hands up to the rim of the
mixing bowl.

He pulled and kicked himself up so
that he could look down and see and
smell the spicy mixture.

"Mmnn, yum!" said Tom. He bent
forward to reach a finger to take a
taste ... and he toppled over the top of
the bowl, plop, into the mix!

If you have ever fallen into an uncooked pudding you will know what sticky stuff it is. It clagged to Tom's arms and clogged to his legs. The more he struggled the more he got stuck in it.

His mother picked up her spoon and slap-slopped the pudding mix, knocking poor Tom dizzy.

Then she scooped the mix, dollop, drop, plop, into a cloth. She tied it tight and popped it into the water to cook.

That water was hot.

"Yeow!" yelled Tom, and he kicked and he struggled.

At last Tom's mother noticed that
her pudding was jumping around and
shouting.

"Bless us all!" she said. "The
pudding's alive! Help!"

And she snatched the pudding
from the pot and she threw it out of
the house and slam-shut the door.

"Ouch!" said Tom as the pudding landed in the grass. Then "Oooer!" because somebody had picked the pudding up.

That somebody was a hungry tinker passing by.

"Well, boggle my eyes, a pudding for free! I'll have that," said the tinker.

"Put me down!" shouted Tom's
teeny-tiny voice. "Let me out!"

"Well, blow me sideways!" said the
tinker. "The dang pudding's alive!" And
he dropped the pudding and he ran.

16

Tom bit with his teeth and he
kicked with his feet and picked with
his fingers. He tore through the
pudding cloth and escaped. He wasn't
far from the cottage ... but a cat was
sniffing close by.

Chapter 3
Goal!

"Ma!" shouted Tom, and he ran on his teeny-tiny legs and he kicked the door as hard as he could, bang, bang, bang.

"Open up, Ma!" he shouted.

"Quick! There's a cat that likes the smell of me!"

Tom's mother opened the door. She
looked in front of her. She looked to
the left and to the right.

"There's nobody there!" she said.
But Tom kicked at her ankle.
"It's me, Ma!"

"Lord love us, it's my darling boy!" said his mother.

She carried Tom safe inside and she bathed him clean in a tea-cup. She told Tom, "From now on, my darling, I'll not let you out of my sight."

After that, Tom was kept indoors.
He got more bored than ever.

He climbed the curtains.

"Get down from there or you'll fall!"
said his mother.

He caught a mouse and took it for
walks on a lead.

"That thing could bite you. You
can't keep it," said his mother.

So Tom stood at the window. The
children outside were playing football.

"Can't I go out and play with them,
Ma?" asked Tom.

"Oo, no, it wouldn't be safe," said
his mother.

Tom scowled and kicked the
window, boom, boom, on the glass to
make his mother as cross as he was.

But one day Tom's Dad said to him,
"Tell you what, lad, why don't I teach
you how to play football like the other
children?"

He took a marble from his pocket
and he put it, plonk, rumble-roll, onto
the table.

"Here, Tom," he said. "Have a kick
of this and see if you can get it
between those two candle sticks. My
finger will be goalie."

Now, a marble on a polished table is
fast. Tom dribbled and darted and
dodged and kicked and scored.
"Goal!" he shouted.

"You're good at this!" said
his Dad.

They played and played.

"I want to play in a team," said Tom.

"I want to play with the children
outside."

"You'll have to ask your mother
about that," said his father.

"Can I, Ma?" asked Tom.

"No, my darling, you cannot."

"Why not?" asked Tom.

"Because," said his mother, "You are teeny-tiny precious. Those other boys might tread on you! No, you stay safe inside with me."

Chapter 4
Oh, Wow!

But one day Tom's mother was in the
doorway, chatting as mothers do.

Tom sneaked out around the
women's ankles.

But as soon as he got outside,
something strong picked Tom up and
lifted him high into the sky.

Tom struggled and twisted and saw that he was in the beak of a big black raven.

"Let go, you bully!" said Tom.

When he looked down he saw his cottage and his Ma shrunk teeny-tiny far away. And he saw great green mountains and a big blue sea that he'd never seen before.

"Oh, wow!" he said.

The raven swooped low as they got
to the sea. It opened its beak and
dropped Tom. He fell, splash-thrash
into salty cold water.

"Oh no," thought Tom. "I'll drown!"

But, as Tom splutter-splashed, a big
fish opened its mouth and gulped. It
swallowed Tom right down into its
dark smelly stomach.

"Oh, Ma," thought Tom. "I wish I'd
stayed safe home with you!"
He curled up small and cried.

But it wasn't long before a
fisherman caught that big fine fish and
he sent the fish to the palace.

The palace cook took one look at
the fish and said, "I'll stuff it full of
herbs, just as King Arthur likes it."
And he took his knife and he slit the
fish – and out stepped Tom Thumb
blinking in the light. He pointed at the
Cook and shouted,

"Put that knife down!"

"Er, yes, Sir," said the Cook, and
he put down the knife.

There was a rare fuss-flurry in the
palace as people told each other the
story of Tom Thumb. Even the King
got to hear it.

"I want to see this teeny-tiny boy,"
said the King.

Chapter 5

What's So Funny?

So Tom was brought, fresh washed and combed.

When King Arthur saw teeny-tiny Tom on his table, he began to laugh. So Tom put his teeny-tiny hands on his teeny-tiny hips and asked, "What's so funny?"

"You are," said King Arthur. "I've never seen anything like you before."

"Well, I've never seen anything like you before either!" said Tom. And he pointed at the king and he laughed. "Hee hee hee, look at him!"

The Palace people were shocked.

"Shall we remove the rude boy?" they asked.

King Arthur shook his head.

"No," he said. "Tom Thumb is right. I am just as much the only king around here as he is the only teeny-tiny boy. It can be lonely being the only one. I could do with a friend who knows how I feel."

"So could I," said Tom.

So the teeny-tiny boy and the great grand king became friends.

King Arthur taught Tom how to behave with dignity. And Tom taught the King how to have fun. He put a hazelnut onto the table.

"Flick that with your finger," said Tom. "See if you can get it past me."

King Arthur got good at dodging and
darting.

"It's even more fun with more
people," said Tom. "You need two
teams to play football properly."

"But where could we get two teams
from?" asked King Arthur.

"There's a team where
I come from," said Tom.

"Come on, then,"
said King Arthur.
"Let's go and
find them."

Chapter 6
Football at The Palace!

So Tom and King Arthur rode over the mountains and fields to Tom's village.

When Tom's mother opened the cottage door she laughed and she cried. She hugged Tom welcome home and she told him off for running away.

At last Tom got free and said,
"Ma, this is my friend, King Arthur."

"Lawks, the King!" said Tom's
mother, and she started laughing and
crying all over again.

The village children came to see
what was going on.

Tom told King Arthur, "These are
my friends, the team."

"Pleased to meet you," said the
King, and the children giggled and
bowed and blushed.

"And this," said Tom, "is my dad.
He's brilliant at teaching football."

So the grown-ups sat and talked
about the weather and drank tea as
grown-ups do. And Tom told the
children all about the King and the
palace and how he came to be there.
"Oh, wow!" they said.

"Would you like to come and play football at the palace and see it for yourself?" asked Tom.

"Yes please!" said the children. "You be our captain, Tom."

So they all travelled back to the palace.

Tom's dad taught the palace people how to kick and tackle and dribble and shoot a ball.

Tom's mother had a chat and tea
with the Queen. And Tom took his
team down to the kitchen to see the
knife that had cut him out of the fish.

Then it was time for the match.
The shouting and cheering and arguing
were much the same as at any football
match you or I have ever seen. But the
pitch was a big round table and the
ball was a glistening pearl.

"Kids against the King? We'll easily win!" Tom told the children. And they did.

"Hooray!"

"Would you like to play again next Saturday?" asked the King.

"Yes please!"

As they trundled home, Tom's
mother said, "You'll never guess what!
The Queen has asked me to sew
some special little clothes for her
baby princess!"

Tom's dad winked at Tom. He said
to his wife, "You'll be busy then.
You won't want Tom under your feet
all day."

"No I won't," agreed Tom's ma.
"You'll just have to go out and
play with the others, Tom."

"Thanks, Ma!" said
Tom, and he scrambled
up onto her shoulder
and kissed her.

About the author

The story of Tom Thumb is the oldest story for children that anybody has found written down. It is a story about a tiny boy and the adventures he has. The story has been written down again and again by different people over hundreds of years. Each of those people has made their own small changes.

I've made a change to the story, too. I've added the finger football bit. It seems to me that finger football is just the right game for a boy who is no bigger than a man's thumb!